This Notebook Belongs To

____

Quick Note

Made in the USA
Las Vegas, NV
03 October 2023

78504748R00068